Blake Salemink

Blake's Nursery Crimes

Blake Salemink

Blake's Nursery Crimes

Nursery Rhymes and Crimes

JustFiction Edition

Imprint

Cover image: www.ingimage.com

Publisher:
JustFiction! Edition
is a trademark of
Dodo Books Indian Ocean Ltd. and OmniScriptum S.R.L Publishing group
Str. Armeneasca 28/1, office 1, Chisinau-2012, Republic of Moldova, Europe
Printed at: see last page
ISBN: 978-613-9-42528-0

Blake’s Nursery Crimes

Table of Contents

To My Sister

Who caringly nursed me from a baby ….

Coca Loca

Totally atrocious

Simply egregious

Time to fly

Locomotive

Light

This little light of mind

I find it to be for the blind

Lightning Comes

Lightning countdown

5,4,3,2,1

Sound comes Sound fades

You shady

I'm Dre

You gay 54321

Rain 2

Out of use

Out of deuce

Rain rain crimes again

Die in vain

Fuck you the same

Little Light

This little light

Might strike

Woody Wood Peacker

Woody

Should he

Chuck a nookie

Blow a wookie

How much wood could a pecker cut if he could peck wood

King Jack

Jack n JIll went up the hill

Jill came down

Smoked a dubious and went around

Ka-blam Jack went tup again and lost his head

Jill came tumbling after

Gauntlent

Your gaunt

So don't front

Okay mont

Twinkle Twinkle

Twinkle twinkle

Winkle winkle

SImply singling

So wrangling

He hee I peed

Nikki Nikki

Nikki Nikkie

Nine doors

Five doors

Seven droors

Sea

Out to sea
You wanna be me
I see this light
It ain[‘t nice

Duel me
I don’t think so
Duel he
He will pee

All i know isthis world
Isn’t great without me

Row row row your boat
Get a moat
Around the goat

Roiw row row your boat
Gently down the stream
Merrily
Merrily
Merrily
Life is a dead fairy

Clown

You a clown
Frown
Brown
You a sad joke
McDona'ds won't give ou a hope
Because you so goat
You damn boat

Lightning

Lighting go away
Thunder Bay is gay
Count to ten
Bend

Eggs

Eggs and Benny
Lenny
Heavenly
I see you score

Becasue green eggs and ham

Are spam

Ice Cream

Ice cream

My cream

Sublime

Verve

Wods nerds

Low leve scrap

Bat trap Smackj ya

Trash ya

Lick ya

Ya done

Ding Dong

Ding Dong

Gone John

Stay Hun

Be guns

I hide because you cry

Chong Chong
Change
You SUck
Bitch
You twitch
Need a switch

Chong Chong Chong
It's over
Red Rover

Holy crap Ijust made revenge on my shoulder
I made it
Ya

Ding Dong
Chong Chong

Pixie Twixie

FDuck your twinkie
Dingie Bingie Simply tweebly

Peanuts

Snoopy

Charlie Brown

Frown

Down Clown

Humpty Dumpty

Nursery the DUmber

The dumpty

He sat on a ledge

Humpty had a big edge

He fell down

And all around people never wanted to put humpty together again

Matrix

Matrix

Hat

Ricks

St

Dicks

Thkning of seeing

Numbers and lines

Controlling the rewind

Yoda

Yoda

Drink some coca cola

Don't go sola

Oops

Solo

Potatoes

One potato, two potato, three potato

Four potatoes, Five potatoes and Six Potatoes

All the rest eat a damn potato

Legend of Tarzan

You are a barzan

Eating tacos at a razon

Simply kinding the rest of half time

Soma a Bratina

Faire a chaque

Faire a chaque

Dome a bratina

Simply tell me what you mean huh?

Cheese

Two cheeks huh

Or put cheese on it

Did somebody say Just Eat?

Marquarita with cheese on it

I get what I want because I want it

Or I put cheese on it

Because you put cheese off it

Ring Around

Ring Around the roses

Or put a hose on you hoses

Ring around the roses

Pocket full of poses

Because you noses

Secretes

Maybe I'm secret
Or secrete
These cigarettes
Don't tell me I'm done
Because these rhymes
Are nursery crimes

Windchimes

Sucka free when I pin rhymes
Rhymes sound like wind chimes
Or like Little guys
It actually sounds like wind chimes
Dimes or mimes

Felon

For he's a jolly good felon
For he's a jolly good felon
And nobody can deny
Unless you lye

Dire straights

Nothing like choirs eh?

Pigs in Blankets

Not by the hair of my chinny chin chin
Till you get my dinner din din
The big bad wolf
Ain't about to gloat
This little pig went to heaven
This little pig went to hell
This little pig went scurrying all the way home
Not by the hair of my chinny chin chin

Smokes

Gimme Gimme's never get
So here's a cigarette
Don't let it bet

To Be

To be nice
Or not to be nice

Roll a dice

Try thrice

Slice

Wise it is

Till I get to him

Blue

Little boy blue and the King in the room, dude

The big grey elephant sat by the dude

And his name was very rude

Sam

Sam I am

Here I'm damned

Sam I am

Green eggs and jam

Cake

Let them eat cake

Let them date

Till you hate

About

And that's what it's all about
Just a couth

Everyone

Everyone owes
Everyone pays
Everyone loans
Everyone is gay

Starlight

Starlight
Starbright
Just right
It's tight
Like a bright spot
Or a dark knot

Humpty Dumpty

Humpty Dumpty sat on a wall
Couldn't put Humpty together again

All the Kings Horses and all the Kings men
Just sat around picking a hen
They sat so long
They thought they were wrong
Until oh my
Humpty Dumpty was broken again

Lions, Bears & Tigers

Oh my
Yes I
I lie
Lions tigers and bears Oh my
Till I die
I will try
To be a lion or a bear or a tiger
Like fries

Lie

I lied

I tried

I died

I spied

Until I cried

Mary

Mary mary quite contrary

She bit an eagle and went off to a fairy

To See

To see or not to see

That is the c

Or a question

Mind your P's and Q's

Don't lie

And remember

To be or not to be

Is the beesiness

Yet the beesiness

Is seasoness

And yes

I want to see

But smell
I melt
Oh no, I delt
Some belts
And now I yelp
For a little freezie
And yet I know
That to be or not to be
Is to see or not to see
I've already told you
In these rhymes
These nursery crimes
That to be nice or not
To be nice
Is just right
Okay
Baby
Ya Lady
I could go on
But these nursery rhymes or crimes
Need to sublime
And be on time
And lie
Yet again
To see or not to see

That is the question
What question I don't know
Yet I know

Square Dancing

You do the hokey pokey and turn yourself around
Then you split an eagle until it frowns
Twice around

Vape

Vape
Date
Hate
Mate
I can't believe this vape

Jare

Cutlery BUtlery
Hiterly Nothingery
Hillary
Suck my Clinton Balls

Hey Bitsy Spider

The Itsy Bitsy Spider
Went up the water spout
Down came the rain
And washed them all abouit
Up came the rain and spit
The spider out
Not it's a itsy bitsy spider
That spit the water out

Butter

Its better with butter
And all the trouble
Double or nothing
He's clarified butter
Make a yorkshire pudding
And put Jam on it
And jodi too
Luke and nuts rub go
We'll make sauce
It's better with butter

Butlery

Butlery
Cutlery
Mutlery
Fuckery
Huttery

Balls

It's all balls
Who's got a biggest balls
Like Hillary said
Suck my clinton balls

Try

I try
Oh I tried
I died
I lied
Now I cry again
Wish

Wish me well

A fairly fellow

But I bellow

Hello

Yellow

Mellow

Okay now delve in

Cherry

If he can't do it

Noone can

Unless you can guess

The cherry

And be merry

A fairy fellow

But I called it yellow

Sharing

Sharing

Caring

Daring

Okay rearing

Honour

For Honur

For smothar

Mother

Barter

Call of Duty

Black Ops Zombie

Fuck you're Mommy

Go home buddy

In

Put the Pin In

Going in with Lucas

Lucas

Hokas

Pokas

Locas

Focus

Eh Choice Is?

$1 Bill

Smaller
Holla
For a dollar
Okay shot colla
Tell me who is baller

Wife Of Bath

Fuck you're horny ass
You just go travel like a sasmarass
Okay now buddy
Go to your hubby
And tell me who is more trouble

Coats

Cords and Coast and Coats
Acordion Coats
Try to tell me I don't rhyme
I tell you the next line
Will be a song about time

Sayings

Come one Come all

To the part of the ball

Festival of Fools

Let Quasimoda go

Jack and the Beanstalk

Hulk

Fuck

Chuckery

Giant Killer

Beanstalk climberr

And alot of highers

Jack Reacher

Jack Rabbit

Black and Yellow

Hello

Sir against

Below fellow

Humble

Be humble
Or Bumble
Sit down
Or go around
Tell me who is surround

Eminem

Eminem Lion Bio
King
Daniel Scarf
Tue. Aug 25
Bio
King
Him
Neil
Heel

Satellites

Satellites or settings

Juices or hats

Sick flowers

Or powers

Skrillex

Skrillex

Dillex

Stillex

Millex

Avicci

Deadmau$

Or dead mouse

Ha

Red house

Or

Bed house

Avicci

Reve

SCH

RCH

Ca Ira

Skyper, Gmail, Tik Tok

Movies, Pics, 8 Mile

Mixup

Electronics are wrong

Magic Gladiator

Superman

Mp3

Cords Chickens

To be or not to be

That is the question

Or rather statement

I hate this

To be nice or not to be nice

Wine are eh nice dice

London Bridge

London Bridge is falling down

Falling down

Now what do you do when it's falling down

Ka-plam

San Francisco is Burnt down

San Fran is burning down

Or well

He's gonna be building up

Until it rots

San Fran is burning down

All the history gone

George 2

George, George

George of the jungle

Tunnel

Hunter

Tell me are you a bunter

London

London Bridge is breaking down

Ca ira

Ca ira

London bridge is falling down

Oh well

London bridge beckons you

La la la la

London bridge is burning down

Down down to the ground

Shower

Shower Shower

Power Power

No, I have you forever

Huggies

Huggies

Puller Ups

The fun of wearing underwear

Oh shit…

Shit…

Moon

Wife of Bath

Oh this trash

Tell me of the moon

Chaucer's Loon

Bite

Don't bite the hand that feeds

Just feed the hand that needs

One or the Other

Jimmy Buffet or Tom Petty

Green Day or U2

Bono

Oh no

Coldplay or the Beatles

Rolling Stones or

Err McJagr

Fuck you lagger

Shakespear or William Blake

Highlander Mollard

Blake

Fate Date Hate

Faces

Faces Fading

Colours Changing

Names Erasing

Fuck

You ask me to

Fuck

you

The deep seated trust

Rubix Cube

Build a deck

Scram You

Kings

Kings never die

But I’m not alike

Am I a king

Or just a ring?

Beef

Got Beef
Eh Thief
Keith Ledger
Hedger
Do Re Mi
Hey Bee
Meatbally
Meatballs & Mushroom
Get be dumped
Feel the world
Like a scourge
Is awful
Yet spaghetti is wet
The meatball rolled off the table
Fable

Late Sunrise

Early sunrise in the morning
Sailor's warning

Nightime's sunrise
Sailor's delight
Oh I forgot to mention
Barn on fire
Stupid tires

Delete

We don't need it
So we can delete it
Suck a little free dik

Easy

Eazy Easy Peezy Peeesy
Japanesey

Uber

Stueber
Duder
Dudeness
Starky and Hutch
Big Lebwoksi

Housekey

Cup

All for a cup
The Stanley Cup
All for a paper
The holy paper

Gladiator

Colloseum
History
Channel
Battle
Tuesday August Thirtieth
I spit the truth
Illest ever

Wayne's World

Lil Wayne
Or Big Wayne
All the same

Eh, Dave

Lewis Capaldi

Olivia Wild
Oscar Wilder
Gene Wilder

Anema

Covid 19 or Chicken Pox
Monkey Pox or Silly Pox

Christmas

Have a holly jolly Chirstmas
Best time of the year
Santa Claus is coming again
So grow a beard and wear red
He knows what you've been doing
So be doing the best thing
Until a tranny pops out
And
Bling Blings

Kramerica Industries

Vandale Industries
Jessica Simpson
Lords of Dogtown

Alcohol

Last call for Alcohol
Shooters are free
Shower Marguritas and Alcohol Tea

Manners

Mind your manners
Forever Life
Outcome Letters
Setting sun
Mind your manners
Got to go over
The rest is closure
Mind your manners
Chiddy Bang

Skrillex

Deal it

Avicci

Deadmau$

Bitch

Ice cream

Or Dis

Ice T

Finnegan’s Wake

Kinda like Jacob’s

But without the dude

A big storm is brewing

For your mate

Kinda like Jacob’s

But without the rain and the storm

Fuck you mate

Finnegan’s Wake

Early Sunrise

Eerly sunrise in the morning

Sailor's warning

Nighttime's Sunrise

Sailor's delight

I forget to mention

Barn's on fire

Stupid tires

All for 1

1 for all

No more

Whore

Do'a think I'll bite

The core

Lore oh no

Horror

House of Horrorshop

Chamber of Horrorshop

But that sourpop

Goes well with slurpees

Oh geez …

Shots

One Shot
2 shot
3 shot
More
4 shot
5 shot
6 shot
Score

Faces

Faces Fading
Colours Changing
Names Erasing

Fuckery

You ask me to
Fuck
You
Then deep you

Rubix Cube

Build a deck
Screw you
Magic dude

Lost Kings

Kings never die
But I’m not alive
Am I a King
Or just a ring?

Humpty Dummy

Humpty Dumpty sat on a wall
Humpty Dumpty had a great fall
Dumpty Buppety Trumpity Thump.
Sir Thump a lot came and put Humpty back together again

Troublesome

Am I trouble
I know I am
But Am I double
I hope I am
I am whatever you say I am
Green cheese and ham

Star

Wish upon a star
Oh my
You are
So are

San Francisco is Burnt down

San Fran is burning down
Or well
He's gonna be building up
Until it rots
San Fran is burning down
All the history gone

What do You

Whatr do you do me now

When do you do when you live in a shoe

Clue or

Do the dew

Dude rude

Tie a lace and make a bow

99 Bottles

99 Bottles of beer on the wall

Take one down

Break it now

Survival

Survival of the strongest

Or the wrongest

To Be 2

To be here or not to be here

I clearly see

Thumpty Turner

DIscombobluated

Hay day

May Day

The Cat

The Cat came back

You thought he was a goner

But the cat came back

And shat on the hat

Rain

Rain rain

Go away

Come again

At the end of the day

Wash

Wash behind your ears

Clean behind your ears

And don’t forget, you’re weird

Mackay

Don’t do drugs mmmackay
Don’t do drugs mmmmkay

Jack Rabbit

The fields are out of reach
And the fields of the countryside
I lie in daisies
I hide in wheat
I lie
Like a damn fly

Learn

First you learn
To walk
The ball
Throw the gall
Then next is to talk
Then you get fucked

Little Boy

Blue and the King of the room
Dude
Your dudeness

Ship

Shape up
Or ship out
Do your pants up
You fucking cunt

Bird

Early bird
Gets teh worm
Late bird
Gets bugger all
Haul the chickens up

Too Little

Too little too late

You stupid gate

Too soon too noon

Tell me its true

Water

Your delinquent daughter

Needs some water

Tell her it's hotter in the summer

Hansens

The Hansens will beat you to a pulp

Tell it all now

bslapshot

Bed Bugs

Sleep tight

Don’t let the bed bugs bite

Fight fight

Dyke dyke

Ice Cream 2

I scream

You scream

We all kill for ice cream

Hiccups

Count to ten

Count to twenty

Fuck up

Ugly

The hiccups ring ups

Now & Then

Faces Fading

Colours Erasing

Names Changing

Smoking or debating

Too

Too little too late
Just because I'm great
So high up with the greats
So close yet so far
All I do is look up at the stars
March on to watergate

American Idiot

Nobody likes you
Everybody hates you
I despise you

Horse

Cart before the horse
Bart before the golf course

Thought

An incomplete thought is all I got
I hope to not

Be left in a rot

Please take my pain and put it aside
So for one day I may be by your side

Tell me if it is okay, that I see you in this way
Don't tell me go go off off and away

Every day is the same
Get up and dress your way

Tell me though if I may
Have some day
To be put away

Biddle

Biddle Widdle Fiddle Kiddle
Think of me was bumble di ka riddle
Don't tell me I'm a little off the fiddle

Tell Me

Tell me what

Don’t get me caught

Yoda 2

Yoda yoda
Drink some Coca Colar

Cola

Cola Cola
Bola Bola
Takes two to dice these
Rhymes and trice these
Coca Loca

Cya (Sia)

Cya later alligator
Wouldn’t wanna be ya
Crocodile
Unless you’re in a gorilla suit
Kangaroo

Huffy Puffy

Huff Huff

Rough rough

Blow your house down

Like I must

Chicken Pot Pie

Chicken pot pie and I don't lie

Why do I cry

At the sound of a fly

ICP or DGK

I see Insane Clown Possy

Or I see Dirty Ghetto Kids

All I see is troublesome

Like in the damn hood

Orange

Orange you glad you found me

Orange you glad I said apple

Orange you glad you had me

Orange you glad I came back

Last Straw

The straw that broke the camel's back

Oh that's wack

Trix

Tricks are for kids

Ok tricks or thinking what I wouldn't do to him

Scrooge

McDuck or get fucked

Rudeus

I'm not rude

Dude

But I hold this sword like it's glue

To stick to you

Trump

Trumpy Dumpy

Humpty

Puffy Dufffy

All the Queen’s men and King’s horses

Couldn’t put Trumpy back together

Bad Boys

Bad Boys

Bad Boys

Whatcha gonna do when they kill you?

WB

Wachowski’s Brothers

In the Matrix

Nuttin’ but luvin

Sunshine (Johnny Cash)

I'll always love you and make you happy,

If you will only say the same.

But if you leave me and love another,

You'll regret it all some day:

Sooner than not the sun will be blue

Like the blue skies
But brighter
Oh Sky, Oh Sun
How are you
Like a hunny bun

I want to hold you but I can't
Because you are so damn

Thanks
The truth is
The sun is where the fun
Is
And my mom said not to
Let a day win
Without dinner or a chance to sing
Oh sunshine

Bald

Bald as an egg
Like Elton John
Just a dumb kid

Noosepaper

Money where my mouth is
The truth is this noosepaper
Is beckoning an end to me
The death of me
Put my money where my money is
Okay now it's gone again
The noosepaper is where
I keep my money
Because it keeps my knowledge
Updates and news
Everything is there
Entertainment
Music
Horoscopes
Oh no horrorscopes

1,000,000

If I had a million dollars
I'd buy a damn museum
And call it hallmark

Wizard

We're off to see the wizard

The wonderful wiard of balls

Flat Tire

Your attitude is like a flat tire
It doesn't get you anywhere
Ok there calm down now
Jacob's son of Baldey Air

Leopard

A leopard doesn't change it's spots
Ok bot
Tell me if you doubt it at all
Dot

Sausages

Sausage & Potatoes
Bubbles and Squeak
Bangers and Smash
Fuck your trash

Printed by Books on Demand GmbH, Norderstedt / Germany